CKD Stage 3

and

Diabetes Type 2

Cookbook

Nutritious Low-Sodium Low-Potassium and Low-Carb Recipes to Reverse Stage 3 Chronic Kidney Disease and Type 2 Diabetes

Alvin Lewis

Disclaimer

The information and recipes provided in this cookbook are intended for general informational purposes only. The author and publisher are not responsible for any adverse effects or consequences resulting from the use or misuse of the content contained herein. Readers are advised to consult with a qualified healthcare professional or nutritionist before making significant dietary changes, especially if they have existing health conditions or concerns.

How to Use This Cookbook

1. **Familiarize yourself with the Cookbook:** Begin by thoroughly reading the introductory sections of this cookbook. Gain an understanding of the philosophy behind the recipes, the nutritional principles, and the overall approach to managing CKD Stage 3 and Type 2 Diabetes. Pay attention to any specific guidelines or recommendations provided.

2. **Evaluate Your Dietary Needs:** Assess your specific dietary needs in light of your Type 2 Diabetes and CKD Stage 3 status. Take note of any restrictions or recommendations mentioned in this cookbook.

3. **Plan Your Meals:** Utilize this cookbook's meal planning section to plan your daily or weekly meals. Consider factors such as variety, nutritional balance, and portion control. This Cookbook also offers sample meal plans, which can help you organize your diet more efficiently. Observe the suggested portion sizes and ingredient pairings.

4. **Try Different Recipes:** Begin incorporating this cookbook's recipes into your daily meals. Start with a

couple of dishes that suit your dietary requirements and taste preferences. Once you feel more at ease, try experimenting with a wider variety of recipes and adhering to the prescribed guidelines.

5. Observe and Modify: Regularly monitor your blood sugar levels, kidney function, and general health as you incorporate this cookbook's recommendations into your daily routine. Pay attention to how your body responds to different meals. Consult your healthcare physician if necessary to make adjustments based on your health progress and any particular worries you may have. Keep in mind that using a cookbook-based strategy is a path towards living a healthier and more energetic lifestyle, not merely a way to manage illnesses.

Table of Contents

More Books from the Author

<u>CKD Stage 4 Cookbook for Seniors</u>

Or Scan the QR code to Access all Books by the Author

Introduction

Sarah, a vibrant and determined woman in her early 50s, who found herself facing the daunting challenge of managing both CKD Stage 3 and Type 2 Diabetes. Sarah felt it was time for a change after becoming frustrated with the restrictions her health issues placed on her day-to-day activities.

Sarah set off on a metamorphosis, driven by her determination to recover her health via a dietary approach. Equipped with knowledge from the "**CKD Stage 3 and Diabetes Type 2 Cookbook**," she began to make intentional and considered meal choices.

Sarah had to first deal with the changes in her eating habits that were unavoidable. She followed the cookbook's guidelines for a healing diet, being mindful of the nutrients she was consuming. She became aware of the significance of keeping her kidneys' ideal fluid intake, controlling her sodium and potassium levels, and balancing her protein intake.

Sarah's meal planning evolved into an artistic endeavor as she included the cookbook's delectable and nutrient-dense recipes. Her go-to meals became quinoa and fresh berries for breakfasts, lentil and vegetable stews for lunches, and grilled fish with lemon-dill sauce for supper.

Most importantly, Sarah knew how important it was to eat at regular intervals and control portions. Sarah learned the value of super foods in sustaining her blood sugar levels and kidney function as she continued on her journey to wellness. Her diet began to include berries, leafy greens, foods high in omega-3 fatty acids, and blood sugar-stabilizing spices like turmeric and cinnamon.

With time, Sarah not only managed but also reversed the progression of CKD Stage 3 and Type 2 Diabetes. Along with her dedication to a healing diet, she made lifestyle adjustments that improved her general health, like managing her stress, getting enough sleep, and exercising frequently.

Today, Sarah is a testament to the transformative impact of embracing the right dietary preferences. Her story inspires others facing similar health challenges, showing them that with determination, knowledge, and the right guidance, it is possible to not just manage but reverse the course of chronic diseases. Sarah's journey stands as a compelling reminder that food can indeed be a powerful form of medicine.

In a world where health often takes a back seat to the demands of daily life, the "**CKD Stage 3 and Diabetes Type 2 Cookbook**" stands as a beacon of hope and empowerment. Picture Sarah—a woman faced with the intricate challenges of managing CKD Stage 3 and Type 2 Diabetes. Her journey, captured within these pages, is not just a narrative but a roadmap to transformation, where the right dietary choices become the catalyst for reclaiming well-being.

Within these chapters, we explore the intricate dance of essential nutrients, revealing the delicate balance required for kidney health and blood sugar control. We dive into the world of meal planning and portion control, making every bite a deliberate step toward better health.

This guide is more than just a recipe book; it's a way of life. It's a tribute to the profound relationship between nutrition and health, showing how making the proper dietary decisions may both prevent and cure chronic illnesses.

Join us on a journey towards a healthier, more vibrant life – one recipe at a time. Your path to wellness unfolds with each turn of the page.

Chapter 1: Understanding Type 2 Diabetes and CKD Stage 3

Type 2 Diabetes and Chronic Kidney Disease (CKD) Stage 3 are two common and related medical disorders that need to be managed with caution and a comprehensive strategy. Let's explore a thorough comprehension of each.

Overview of Stage 3 Chronic Kidney Disease (CKD)

The increasing loss of kidney function over time is a hallmark of chronic kidney disease (CKD). Stage 3 is a crucial point where there is a moderate impairment in kidney function. During this stage, kidneys struggle to filter waste and excess fluids effectively. Common indicators include elevated blood pressure, abnormal levels of electrolytes, and the presence of protein in the urine.

Recognizing potential causes of CKD Stage 3, such as genetic predisposition, diabetes, and hypertension, is essential to understanding the condition. A multimodal strategy, involving dietary and lifestyle alterations, is necessary for managing stage 3 CKD. Patients frequently need to maintain appropriate hydration levels while controlling their sodium, potassium, and protein intake. The objective is to lessen the progression of kidney damage and mitigate associated complications.

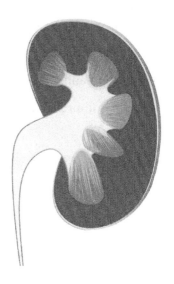

Overview of Diabetes Type 2

Type 2 Diabetes is a metabolic disorder characterized by insulin resistance, where the body's cells don't respond effectively to insulin. Elevated blood sugar levels result from this. Diabetes increases the risk of chronic kidney disease (CKD) because it damages the kidneys' tiny blood capillaries.

Understanding Type 2 Diabetes entails realizing the significance of regulating blood sugar levels via food adjustments, medication, and lifestyle adjustments. Eating a well-balanced diet rich in fiber, lean proteins, complex carbohydrates, and healthy fats will help control blood sugar levels.

Relationship between Type 2 Diabetes and Stage 3 CKD

Type 2 Diabetes and CKD frequently coexist, posing difficult health issues. Diabetes is a major contributor to CKD, and CKD can make problems from diabetes worse. Coordinated management of both diseases is necessary, with dietary choices playing a pivotal role.

Nutritional Strategies

Understanding CKD Stage 3 and Type 2 Diabetes involves adopting a kidney-friendly and diabetes-appropriate diet. This entails keeping an eye on nutrient consumption, controlling portion sizes, and including foods that aid with blood sugar regulation and kidney function.

The "**CKD Stage 3 and Diabetes Type 2 Cookbook**" offers helpful advice on how to prepare meals that not only please palates but also improve the general health of individuals dealing with these medical issues.

Adopting a diet rich in nutrients and well-balanced is essential for controlling and, in certain situations, even reverses the effects of Type 2 Diabetes and CKD Stage 3.

Chapter 2: Foundations of a Healing Diet

A healing diet is the cornerstone of a transforming path toward better health and well-being in the complex world of controlling Type 2 Diabetes and Chronic Kidney Disease (CKD) Stage 3. This section explores the fundamental principles that guide individuals on this path, providing insights into the synergy between nutrition, kidney health, and blood sugar control.

Nutrition's Role in Diabetes and CKD Management

Understanding the critical role nutrition plays in managing Type 2 Diabetes and Stage 3 CKD is at the heart of the healing process. Nutrition is a strategic tool that enables individuals to take charge of their health outcomes; it's not just about tracking calories. A healing diet becomes more than just sustenance for individuals with diabetes and chronic kidney disease (CKD); it becomes medication.

In CKD Stage 3, where the kidneys are moderately impaired, careful consideration of nutrient intake becomes crucial. Particularly to be concerned with are potassium, sodium, and protein. A healing diet involves a delicate balance, ensuring adequate nourishment while minimizing the strain on the kidneys. Knowing how these nutrients affect kidney function is essential to preparing meals that nourish these essential organs rather than overload them.

For individuals with Type 2 Diabetes, blood sugar regulation becomes more important. The focus is primarily on the quantity and quality of carbohydrates. Choosing complex carbs over simple sugars, controlling the glycemic index and load, and using fiber to slow down glucose absorption are all part of a healing diet for diabetes. The symbiotic relationship between nutrition and blood sugar control is a central theme in the foundations of this healing diet.

Essential Nutrients for Kidney Health

A sophisticated approach to nutrient intake is necessary to navigate CKD Stage 3. Traditionally a staple of the diet, proteins must be controlled. A CKD healing diet includes limiting intake and choosing high-quality protein sources to lessen the strain on the kidneys. Dietary protein recommendations may vary based on individual factors, emphasizing the need for personalized dietary plans.

Another crucial element is sodium management. High sodium levels can contribute to fluid retention and increased blood pressure, placing additional strain on compromised kidneys. A healing diet demands close monitoring of sodium consumption, which is frequently achieved through reduction of processed meals and incorporation of fresh, whole foods that are cooked with little to no salt.

Potassium level regulation is similarly important. High potassium levels, which are common in CKD, can cause dangerous heart rhythms.

A healing diet allows people to enjoy a variety of nutrient-dense meals without jeopardizing kidney health by carefully choosing fruits and vegetables with moderate potassium content.

Maintaining Carbohydrate Balance for Diabetes Control

The key to a successful healing diet for Type 2 Diabetes is learning how to balance your intake of carbohydrates. Since carbohydrates have a direct effect on blood sugar levels, both their quantity and quality are essential for managing diabetes.

It becomes essential to comprehend glycemic load (GL) and glycemic index (GI). While the GL takes into account both the quality and quantity of Carbohydrates taken, the GI gauges how rapidly a diet containing carbohydrates elevates blood glucose. A healing diet for diabetes encourages the selection of low-GI and low-GL foods, promoting stable blood sugar levels and reducing the risk of diabetes related complications.

In the dietary narrative of diabetes, fiber emerges as the hero. Fiber, which is present in whole grains, legumes, fruits, and vegetables, not only slows down the absorption of glucose but also promotes satiety, aiding in weight management—a significant factor in diabetes control.

Importance of Fluid Consumption

The often-overlooked component of fluid consumption is addressed in a healing diet for diabetes and CKD. Sufficient hydration promotes general health and is essential for renal function. However, individuals with CKD may need to monitor their fluid intake more closely, as impaired kidneys may struggle to excrete excess fluids, leading to edema and high blood pressure.

In summary, a thorough grasp of the complex relationship between nutrition, kidney health, and blood sugar regulation forms the basis of a healing diet for CKD Stage 3 and Type 2 Diabetes. It entails making thoughtful decisions, individualized changes, and a dedication to utilizing food as an effective instrument in the pursuit of better health. The "CKD Stage 3 and Diabetes Type 2 Cookbook" is a beacon of hope, showing the way toward an all-encompassing healing diet that embraces the diverse range of scrumptious and nourishing foods that enhance the body's natural ability to mend and flourish.

Chapter 3: Meal Planning and Portion Control

Meal planning and portion management become crucial cornerstones of a comprehensive approach to nutrition in the complex dance of controlling Type 2 Diabetes and CKD Stage 3. These practices go beyond mere dietary strategies; they become the blueprint for wellness, shaping the way individuals nourish their bodies to support kidney health and blood sugar control.

Preparing Well-Balanced Meals for Diabetes and CKD

Planning meals for those with CKD and diabetes requires careful consideration of how to create nutrient-dense, well-balanced meals that meet the specific requirements of each disease. The cornerstone is choosing a range of foods high in vital nutrients while considering the specific dietary restrictions associated with CKD Stage 3 and Type 2 Diabetes.

For CKD, the focus is on managing protein, sodium, and potassium intake. A well-planned meal plan eliminates processed meals rich in sodium and includes high-quality proteins such lean meats and poultry. It emphasizes fresh fruits and vegetables with moderate potassium content, striking a delicate balance to nourish the body without overburdening the kidneys.

Meal planning for diabetics is all about limiting carbohydrates to keep blood sugar levels steady. Whole grains, fiber, and complex Carbohydrates are encouraged components of the healing diet.

Importance of Regular Eating Times

Timing meals consistently is essential to treating diabetes and CKD. Frequent eating periods help distribute nutrient intake throughout the day and support stable blood sugar levels. This practice helps prevent extreme fluctuations in blood glucose, promoting overall metabolic health.

Regular eating schedules are important for maintaining fluid balance and avoiding needless renal strain for individuals with CKD. It makes it possible to consume fluids more consistently, which supports the delicate equilibrium needed for kidney function.

Chapter 4: Super Foods for Kidney and Blood Sugar Health

Super food integration is a potent tactic to support kidney function and regulate blood sugar levels in the complex management of Chronic Kidney Disease (CKD) Stage 3 and Type 2 Diabetes. In addition to providing an abundance of vitamins, minerals, and antioxidants, these nutrient-dense meals are essential for maintaining the complex dance between glucose management and renal function.

Kidney-Friendly Superfoods

1. **Berries, Cherries, and Apples:** Berries, such as blueberries, strawberries, and raspberries, are rich in antioxidants, particularly anthocyanin, which have been linked to improved kidney function. Because of its anti-inflammatory qualities, cherries may help lessen the kidneys' oxidative stress. Apples, high in fiber and antioxidants, contribute to blood sugar stability, making them a versatile and kidney-friendly fruit choice.

2. Cruciferous vegetables and leafy greens: Nutrient-dense leafy greens, such as spinach, kale, and Swiss chard, are excellent sources of folate and vitamin K. These vegetables are low in potassium, making them ideal for individuals with CKD. Broccoli and cauliflower are examples of cruciferous vegetables that are low in potassium and contain substances that may have an anti-inflammatory impact, which helps maintain healthy kidneys and control blood sugar levels.

3. Omega-3 Rich Foods: Salmon, mackerel, and trout are examples of fatty fish that are high in omega-3 fatty acids. Because of their anti-inflammatory qualities, these important fats help control diabetes and maintain kidney health. By lowering kidney inflammation and increasing insulin sensitivity, omega-3s may help manage Type 2 Diabetes and Chronic Kidney Disease concurrently.

Blood Sugar Stabilizing Super Foods

1. Cinnamon, ginger, and turmeric: These spices have antioxidant and anti-inflammatory qualities. Turmeric, with its active compound curcumin, may contribute to kidney health, while ginger and cinnamon have been associated with improved insulin sensitivity and blood sugar control.

2. Nuts and Seeds: Almonds, walnuts, flaxseeds, and chia seeds are rich in healthy fats, fiber, and essential nutrients. These super foods help regulate blood sugar, lower inflammation, and support heart health in addition to providing a satisfying crunch.

Chapter 5: Delicious and Nutrient-Packed Recipes

10 Breakfast Recipes

Quinoa and Berry Breakfast Bowl

Cooking & Prep Time: 20 minutes

Ingredients:

- 1/2 cup rinsed quinoa
- 1 cup of water
- 1/2 cup mixed berries (raspberries, strawberries, and blueberries)
- 1 teaspoon honey, if desired
- 1 tablespoon chopped almonds

Guidelines:

1. Boil water in a saucepan.

2. Add quinoa, lower the heat, cover, and simmer for 15 minutes or until water is absorbed.

3. Fluff quinoa with a fork then transfer to a bowl.

4. Add chopped almonds and mixed berries to top, and if desired, sprinkle with honey.

Spinach and Feta Omelette

Cooking & Prep Time: 10 minutes

Ingredients:

- 2 big eggs
- 1 cup freshly chopped spinach
- 2 tablespoons crumbled feta cheese.
- To taste, add salt and pepper.
- 1 teaspoon olive oil.

1. In a bowl, whisk eggs and season with salt and pepper.

2. In a non-stick skillet, heat the olive oil over medium heat.

3. Add chopped spinach and sauté until it wilts.

4. Pour whisk eggs over spinach, top with feta, and cook until the edges are set.

5. Flip the omelette and cook until it is through.

Blueberry and Whole Grain Pancakes

Cooking & Prep Time: 15 minutes

Ingredients:

- 1/4 cup oats
- 1/2 cup whole wheat flour
- 1/2 teaspoon baking powder
- 1/2 cup milk (plant-based or dairy)
- 1/2 cup fresh blueberries
- 1 tablespoon maple syrup

Guidelines:

1. Combine baking powder, oats, and whole wheat flour in a bowl.

2. Add the milk and maple syrup, and mix thoroughly.

3. Fold in fresh blueberries.

4. Over a medium heat, heat a nonstick skillet or griddle.

5. Pour batter onto the griddle, flipping when bubbles form.

Smoothie Bowl with Mixed Berries and Granola

Cooking & Prep Time: 5 minutes

Ingredients:

- 1/2 cup mixed berries (raspberries, blueberries, and strawberries)
- 1/2 frozen banana
- 1/2 cup Greek yogurt
- 1/4 cup granola
- 1 tablespoon chia seeds

Guidelines:

1. Blend frozen banana, Greek yogurt, and mixed berries in a blender until smooth.
2. Transfer the smoothie to a bowl.
3. Add granola and sprinkle chia seeds.

Avocado and Tomato Breakfast Toast

Cooking & Prep Time: 5 minutes

Ingredients:

- 1/2 ripe avocado, mashed
- 1 slice whole grain bread
- 1 little tomato, sliced

- Season with salt and pepper
- Garnish with fresh basil leaves

Guidelines:

1. Toast the whole grain bread slice.

2. Spread mashed avocado evenly on the toast.

3. Place sliced tomatoes on top.

4. Sprinkle a dash of pepper and salt, and top with some fresh basil leaves.

Cottage Cheese and Pineapple Parfait

Cooking & Prep Time: 5 minutes

Ingredients:

- 1/2 cup cottage cheese low-fat
- 1/2 cup fresh chunks
- 2 tablespoons cereal
- 1 teaspoon honey, if desired

Guidelines:

1. Layer cottage cheese in a bowl or glass.

2. Add chunks of fresh pineapple on top.

3. Sprinkle granola over the pineapple.

4. If desired, drizzle with honey.

Chia Seed Pudding with Berries

Prep Time: 2 hours (mostly refrigeration time)

Ingredients:

- 2 teaspoons chia seeds
- 1/2 cup almond milk
- 1/2 cup mixed berries (strawberries and blueberries)
- 1/2 teaspoon vanilla extract
- 1 tablespoon almonds, sliced

Guidelines:

1. Combine almond milk, vanilla extract, and chia seeds in a bowl.

2. To thicken, let it sit in the refrigerator for at least 2 hours or overnight.

3. Give the mixture a good stir and transfer to a serving bowl.

4. Top with sliced almonds and mixed berries.

Egg White and Vegetable Scramble

Cooking & Prep Time: 10 minutes

Ingredients:

- 3 egg whites
- 1/2 cup diced bell peppers
- 1/4 cup finely sliced red onion
- 1/4 cup chopped cherry tomatoes
- Fresh parsley for garnish
- Season with salt and pepper

Guidelines:

1. Whisk egg whites in a bowl and season with pepper and salt.

2. Sauté red onion and bell peppers in a nonstick skillet until tender.

3. Add the egg whites to the skillet and scramble until cooked.

4. Add cherry tomatoes and cook for an additional minute.

5. Before serving, garnish with fresh parsley.

Greek Yogurt and Berry Smoothie

Cooking & Prep Time: 5 minutes

Ingredients:

- 1/2 cup Greek yogurt
- 1/2 cup mixed berries (raspberries and blueberries)
- 1/2 frozen banana
- 1 tablespoon almond butter
- 1/2 cup almond milk or water

Guidelines:

1. Combine frozen banana, mixed berries, Greek yogurt, almond butter, water or almond milk in a blender.

2. Blend until smooth.

3. Transfer to a glass and savor.

Buckwheat Pancakes with Cinnamon Apples

Cooking & Prep Time: 15 minutes

Ingredients:

- 1/2 cup buckwheat flour
- 1/2 teaspoon baking powder
- 1/2 cup almond milk
- 1/2 teaspoon vanilla extract

- 1 thinly slice medium apple
- 1/2 teaspoon cinnamon

Guidelines:

1. Combine buckwheat flour, baking powder, almond milk, and vanilla extract in a bowl and whisk until well smooth.

2. Heat a griddle or non-stick skillet over medium heat.

3. Spoon batter onto the griddle and flipping when bubbles form.

4. Sauté apple slices with cinnamon in a different pan until Softened.

5. Before serving, top pancakes with cinnamon apples

These breakfast recipes provide variety and creativity for individuals managing CKD Stage 3 and Type 2 Diabetes. Each recipe is carefully designed to balance flavors, textures, and nutritional benefits, ensuring a delightful and nourishing breakfast experience. These recipes showcase the versatility of ingredients within the constraints of a kidney-friendly and diabetes-conscious diet.

Grilled Chicken Salad with Balsamic Vinaigrette

Cooking & Prep Time: 15 minutes

Ingredients:

- 4 ounces skinless, boneless chicken breast
- 2 cups mixed green salad
- 1/2 cup cherry tomatoes, halved
- 1/4 cup sliced cucumber
- 1/4 cup diced red bell pepper
- 1 tablespoon olive oil
- 1 teaspoon balsamic vinegar
- Toppings of salt and pepper

Guidelines:

1. Sprinkle chicken breast with salt and pepper.

2. Cook the chicken on the grill for (5 to 7 minutes on each side), or until it is cooked thoroughly.

3. Combine the red bell pepper, cucumber, cherry tomatoes, and salad greens in a bowl.

4. Slice the grilled chicken and arrange it over the salad.

5. To make the dressing, mix together the olive oil and balsamic vinegar in a small bowl.

6. Drizzle the dressing over the salad before serving.

Quinoa and Chickpea Salad with Lemon-Tahini Dressing

Cooking Time: 20 minutes

Ingredients:

- 1 cup water
- 1/2 cup rinsed quinoa
- 1/2 cup rinsed and drained canned chickpeas
- 1/4 cup finely chopped red onion
- 1/4 cup diced cucumber
- 2 tablespoons chopped fresh parsley

- 2 tablespoons tahini
- Juice of 1 lemon
- To taste, add salt and pepper.

1. Boil water in a saucepan.

2. Add quinoa, lower the heat, cover, and simmer for 15 minutes or until water is absorbed.

3. Combine the cooked quinoa, cucumber, red onion, chickpeas, and parsley in a bowl.

4. To make the dressing, whisk together tahini, lemon juice, salt, and pepper in a small bowl.

5. Before serving, drizzle the salad with the dressing and toss.

Turkey and Avocado Wrap with Greek Yogurt Sauce

Cooking Time: 10 minutes

Ingredients:

- 1 whole wheat tortilla
- 4 ounces thinly sliced lean turkey breast
- 1/4 sliced avocado
- 1/4 cup halved cherry tomatoes

- 1/4 cup young spinach leaves
- 2 tsp. Greek yogurt
- 1/2 teaspoon Dijon mustard
- Toppings of salt and pepper

Guidelines:

1. Cook turkey breast slices in a skillet until thoroughly cooked.

2. Warm the whole wheat tortilla.

3. Cover the tortilla with a layer of Greek yogurt and Dijon mustard.

4. Layer spinach, cherry tomatoes, avocado, and sliced turkey.

5. Season with salt and pepper, then wrap the tortilla.

Mediterranean Quinoa Bowl with Lemon-Herb Dressing

Cooking Time: 20 minutes

Ingredients:

- 1 cup water
- 1/2 cup rinsed quinoa
- 1/4 cup sliced Kalamata olives
- 1/2 cup chopped cucumber

- 1/4 cup crumbled feta cheese
- 1/4 cup halved cherry tomatoes
- 2 teaspoons finely chopped fresh mint
- 2 tablespoons extra virgin olive oil
- 1 lemon's juice
- To taste, add salt and pepper.

1. Boil water in a saucepan.

2. Add quinoa, lower the heat, cover, and simmer for 15 minutes or until water is absorbed.

3. Combine cooked quinoa, cucumber, cherry tomatoes, feta cheese, olives, and mint in a bowl.

4. To make the dressing, whisk together olive oil, lemon juice, salt, and pepper in a small bowl.

5. Before serving, drizzle the dressing over the quinoa bowl and stir.

Salmon and Asparagus Foil Packets

Cooking Time: 20 minutes

Ingredients:

- 4 ounces salmon fillet
- 1/2 cup trimmed asparagus
- 1 tablespoon olive oil
- 1/4 cup halved cherry tomatoes
- 1 tablespoon chopped fresh dill
- Salt and pepper to taste

1. Preheat the oven to 400°F (200°C).

2. Lay a foil-covered salmon fillet on top of it.

3. Place cherry tomatoes and asparagus around the salmon.

4. Drizzle the ingredients with olive oil and season with salt, pepper, and fresh dill.

5. Fold the foil to create a packet and bake for 15-20 minutes until salmon is cooked.

Lentil and Vegetable Stir-Fry

Cooking Time: 15 minutes

- 1/2 cup cooked dried lentils
- 1/2 cup broccoli florets
- 1/2 cup sliced bell peppers
- 1/4 cup carrots, julienned
- 2 teaspoons (low-sodium) soy sauce
- 1 tsp. of sesame oil
- 1 tablespoon minced ginger

Guidelines:

1. Prepare lentils as directed on the packet.

2. Heat the sesame oil in a wok or skillet and stir-fry carrots, bell peppers, and broccoli until crisp-tender.

3. Add minced ginger and cooked lentils to the stir-fry.

4. Drizzle the mixture with soy sauce and mix thoroughly.

Caprese Quinoa Salad

Cooking Time: 20 minutes

Ingredients:

- 1 cup water
- 1/2 cup rinsed quinoa
- 1/4 cup chopped fresh mozzarella

- 1/2 cup cherry tomatoes, halved
- 1 tablespoon balsamic vinegar
- 1 tablespoon olive oil
- 2 tablespoon freshly chopped basil
- To taste, add salt and pepper.

Guidelines:

1. Boil water in a saucepan.

2. Add quinoa, lower the heat, cover, and simmer for 15 minutes or until water is absorbed.

3. Combine cooked quinoa, fresh mozzarella, basil, and cherry tomatoes in a bowl.

4. To make the dressing, combine the olive oil, salt, pepper, and balsamic vinegar in a small bowl.

5. Drizzle the dressing over the salad and toss before serving.

Turkey and Vegetable Skewers

Cooking Time: 15 minutes

Ingredients:

- 1/2 bell pepper, cut into bits
- 4 ounces lean turkey breast, cut into cubes
- 1/2 zucchini, sliced
- 1/4 red onion, thinly sliced

- 1 teaspoon dried oregano
- 1 tablespoon of olive oil
- To taste, add salt and pepper.

1. Preheat a grill or grill pan over medium-high heat.

2. Thread bell pepper, zucchini, red onion, and turkey cubes onto skewers.

3. Combine olive oil, salt, pepper, and dried oregano in a bowl for marinade

4. Apply the marinade to the skewers.

5. Grill the skewers for about 10 minutes, turning occasionally, until turkey is cooked.

Black Bean and Vegetable Wrap

Cooking Time: 10 minutes

Ingredients:

- 1/2 cup rinsed and drained canned black beans
- 1/4 cup diced red bell pepper
- 1/4 cup (fresh or frozen) corn kernels
- 1/4 cup diced avocado
- 1 whole-wheat tortilla
- 1 tablespoon salsa
- 1 tablespoon chopped cilantro

1. Combine black beans, corn, avocado, and red bell pepper in a bowl.

2. Warm the whole wheat tortilla.

3. Cover the tortilla with the bean and vegetable mixture.

4. Add salsa and sprinkle chopped cilantro to top.

5. Roll up the tortilla into a wrap.

Vegetarian Chickpea and Spinach Curry

Cooking Time: 15 minutes

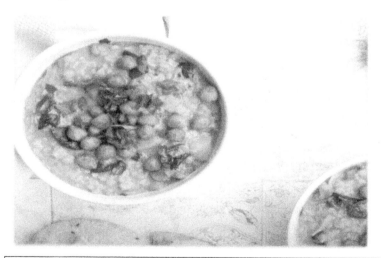

- 1 can (15 oz.) rinsed and drained chickpeas

- 1 cup fresh spinach leaves

- 1/2 cup diced tomatoes

- 1/4 cup chopped onion

- 2 minced garlic cloves

- 1 teaspoon grated ginger

- 1 tablespoon olive oil

- 1 one tablespoon curry powder

- To taste, add salt and pepper.

Guidelines:

1. In a pan, heat olive oil over medium heat.

2. Add grated ginger, diced onion, and garlic. Sauté until aromatic.

3. Add diced tomatoes and cook until tender.

4. Add curry powder, salt, pepper, and chickpeas. Simmer for 5 to 7 minutes.

5. Fold in fresh spinach and cook until wilted.

These lunch recipes are designed to be kidney-friendly and suitable for individuals with Type 2 Diabetes. They incorporate nutrient-dense ingredients while considering dietary restrictions associated with CKD Stage 3 and diabetes.

Baked Salmon with Lemon-Herb Quinoa

Cooking Time: 25 minutes

Ingredients:

- 1/2 cup rinsed quinoa
- 1 cup water
- 1 tablespoon olive oil
- 1 salmon fillet (6 oz.)
- 1 teaspoon lemon zest
- 1 tablespoon chopped fresh dill
- Salt and pepper to taste

Guidelines:

1. Preheat the oven to 375°F (190°C).

2. Season the salmon fillet with salt, pepper, and a drizzle of olive oil.

3. Place the salmon in a baking dish and bake it for 15 to 20 minutes, or until it is done.

4. In a saucepan, bring water to a boil, add quinoa, lower heat, cover, and simmer for 15 minutes.

5. Using a fork, fluff the quinoa and mix in olive oil, lemon zest, fresh dill, salt, and pepper.

6. Serve the baked salmon over the lemon-herb quinoa.

Grilled Chicken with Roasted Vegetables

Cooking Time: 30 minutes

Ingredients:

- 1 (6-ounce) chicken breast
- 1 cup broccoli florets
- 1/2 cup halved cherry tomatoes
- 1/2 cup sliced bell peppers
- 1 teaspoon dried oregano
- 1 teaspoon garlic powder
- 1 tablespoon olive oil
- To taste, add salt and pepper.

Guidelines:

1. Over medium-high heat, preheat the grill or grill pan.

2. Sprinkle salt, pepper, garlic powder, and dried oregano to the chicken breast for seasoning.

3. Mix bell peppers, broccoli, and cherry tomatoes in a bowl and toss with olive oil, salt, and pepper.

4. Grill the chicken for 6 to 8 minutes on each side until thoroughly cooked.

5. Roast the vegetables for 15 to 20 minutes in the oven at 400°F (200°C).

6. Serve the roasted vegetables with the grilled chicken.

Vegetarian Eggplant and Chickpea Stew

Cooking Time: 30 minutes

Ingredients:

- 1 can (15 oz.) drained and rinsed chickpeas
- 1 medium eggplant, diced
- 1 cup diced tomatoes
- 1/2 cup chopped onion
- 2 minced garlic cloves
- 1 teaspoon paprika
- 1 teaspoon cumin
- 1 tablespoon olive oil
- 1/4 teaspoon cayenne pepper
- To taste, add salt and pepper.

Guidelines:

1. In a large pot, heat olive oil over medium heat.

2. Sauté minced garlic and onion until tender.

3. Add diced eggplant, tomatoes, chickpeas, paprika, cumin, cayenne, salt, and pepper.

4. Cover and simmer for 20 to 25 minutes or until the eggplant is softened.

5. Before serving, make any necessary spice adjustments.

Shrimp and Zucchini Stir-Fry

Cooking Time: 20 minutes

Ingredients:

- 8 ounces peeled and deveined shrimp
- 2 sliced zucchini
- 1/2 cup trimmed snap peas
- 1/4 cup (low-sodium) soy sauce
- 1 tablespoon sesame oil
- 1 tablespoon grated ginger
- 2 minced garlic cloves
- 1 tablespoon olive oil
- Garnish with sesame seeds

Guidelines:

1. Heat olive oil in a wok or skillet over medium-high heat.

2. Stir-fry the shrimp until they turn opaque and pink. Take out of the pan.

3. In the same pan, add sesame oil, ginger, and garlic. Sauté for 1-2 minutes.

4. Add zucchini and snap peas, stir-fry until the veggies are soft.

5. Put the shrimp back in the pan, Stir in soy sauce, and toss to coat completely.

6. Before serving, garnish with sesame seeds.

Turkey and Vegetable Skillet

Cooking Time: 20 minutes

Ingredients:

- 4 ounces lean ground turkey
- 1/2 cup diced bell peppers
- 1/2 cup sliced zucchini
- 1/4 cup chopped red onion
- 1 tablespoon olive oil
- 1 cup spinach leaves
- 1 teaspoon Italian seasoning
- To taste, add salt and pepper.

Guidelines:

1. In a skillet, heat olive oil over medium heat.

2. Add ground turkey and cook until browned.

3. Add red onion, zucchini, and bell peppers. Sauté until the veggies are softened.

4. Stir in spinach, salt, pepper, and Italian seasoning. Cook until wilted.

Stuffed Bell Peppers with Quinoa and Black Beans

Cooking Time: 35 minutes

Ingredients:

- 2 bell peppers, halved and seeds removed
- 1/2 cup cook quinoa
- 1/2 cup black beans, canned and drained
- 1/4 cup diced tomatoes
- 1/4 cup finely chopped red onion
- 1/2 teaspoon cumin
- 1/2 teaspoon chili powder
- 1/4 cup corn kernels (either fresh or frozen)
- 2 teaspoons chopped fresh cilantro

Guidelines:

1. Preheat the oven to 375°F (190°C).

2. Combine cooked quinoa, cilantro, cumin, chili powder, tomatoes, red onion, black beans, and corn in a bowl.

3. Stuff each bell pepper half with the quinoa mixture.

4. Bake in the oven for 25 to 30 minutes, or until peppers are soft.

Mushroom and Spinach Frittata

Cooking Time: 20 minutes

> *Ingredients:*

- 4 big eggs
- 1 cup sliced mushrooms
- 1 cup fresh spinach leaves
- 1/4 cup crumbled feta cheese
- 1/4 cup diced red bell pepper
- 1 tablespoon olive oil
- To taste, add salt and pepper.

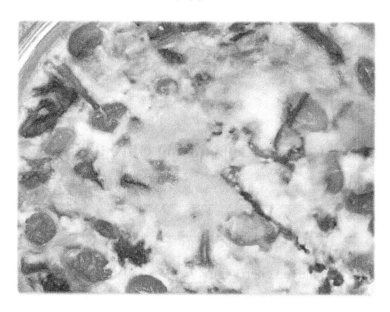

1. Preheat the oven broiler.

2. Heat the olive oil in an oven-safe skillet over a medium heat.

3. Add red bell pepper and mushrooms, sauté until tender.

4. Add spinach and cook until it wilts.

5. Whisk eggs in a bowl, sprinkle with pepper and salt, and pour the mixture over the veggies.

6. Sprinkle crumbled feta on top and cook on the stovetop until the edges set.

7. Transfer the skillet to the oven and broil the frittata until it is well cooked.

Baked Cod with Tomato and Olive Relish

Cooking Time: 25 minutes

Ingredients:

- 2 cod fillets (6 ounces each)
- 1 cup halved cherry tomatoes
- 1/4 cup sliced Kalamata olives
- 1 tablespoon each olive oil
- 1 tablespoon balsamic vinegar

- 2 tablespoon finely chopped red onion
- 1 teaspoon dried oregano
- To taste, add salt and pepper.

Guidelines:

1. Preheat the oven to 400°F (200°C).

2. Season cod fillets with salt, pepper, and dried oregano.

3. Place cod fillets in a baking dish.

4. Combine cherry tomatoes, red onion, olive oil, balsamic vinegar, and Kalamata olives in a bowl.

5. Drizzle the fish fillets with the tomato and olive mixture.

6. Bake in the oven for 15-20 minutes until the cod is flaky.

Vegetarian Lentil Soup

Cooking Time: 30 minutes

Ingredients:

- 1 cup rinsed and dried green lentils
- 1/2 cup chopped carrots
- 1/2 cup chopped celery
- 1/2 cup chopped onion
- 2 minced garlic cloves
- 1 can (14-oz) diced tomatoes

- 4 cups (low-sodium) vegetable broth
- 1 teaspoon paprika
- 1 teaspoon cumin
- 1/2 teaspoon turmeric
- Toppings of salt and pepper
- Fresh parsley for garnish

Guidelines:

1. Sauté onion and garlic in a big pot until tender

2. Add celery, carrots, paprika, cumin, and turmeric. Stir for 2 to 3 minutes.

3. Add lentils and pour in the vegetable broth.

4. Bring to a boil, then reduce the heat, cover, and simmer for 20-25 minutes or until lentils are softened.

5. Add diced tomatoes, then cook for further 5 minutes.

6. Before serving, add salt and pepper to taste and garnish with fresh parsley.

Chicken and Vegetable Stir-Fry with Brown Rice

Cooking Time: 25 minutes

Ingredients:

- 4 ounces thinly sliced, skinless, boneless chicken breast
- 1/2 cup broccoli florets
- 1/2 cup trimmed snap peas
- 1/4 cup (low-sodium) soy sauce
- 1/2 cup julienned carrots
- 1 tablespoon sesame oil
- 1 tablespoon grated ginger
- 2 minced garlic cloves
- 1 cup brown rice, cooked

Guidelines:

1. In a wok or skillet, heat sesame oil over medium-high heat.

2. Stir-fry chicken until browned and thoroughly cooked. Remove from the pan.

3. Add garlic and ginger to the same pan. Sauté for a minute or 2.

4. Add carrots, snap peas, and broccoli. Stir-fry the veggies until they are crisp-tender.

5. Put the cooked chicken back into the pan, pour soy sauce into the mixture and toss to coat well.

6. Spoon cooked brown rice over the stir-fried chicken and vegetables.

Greek Yogurt Parfait with Berries

Cooking Time: 5 minutes

Ingredients:

- 1 cup (low-fat) Greek yogurt
- 1/2 cup mixed berries (strawberries and blueberries)
- 2 tablespoons granola
- 1 teaspoon honey, if desired

Guidelines:

1. Layer Greek yogurt in a bowl or glass.

2. Top with mixed berries.

3. Sprinkle granola over the berries.

4. If desired, drizzle with honey.

Baked Apple Slices with Cinnamon

Cooking Time: 20 minutes

Ingredients:

- 1/2 teaspoon cinnamon
- 1 apple, cored and thinly sliced
- 1 teaspoon heated coconut oil
- 1 teaspoon honey, if desired

Guidelines:

1. Preheat the oven to 375°F (190°C).

2. Mix cinnamon and melted coconut oil in a bowl with apple slices.

3. Place the slices in a single layer on a baking pan.

4. Bake the apples for 15 to 20 minutes, or until softened.

5. Before serving, drizzle with honey if preferred.

Avocado Chocolate Mousse

Prep Time: 10 minutes

Ingredients:

- 1 ripe avocado
- 2 tablespoons unsweetened cocoa powder
- 3 tsp. maple syrup
- 1/2 teaspoon vanilla extract

Guidelines:

1. Scoop the avocado into a food processor or blender.

2. Add vanilla extract, maple syrup, and cocoa powder.

3. Blend until creamy and smooth.

4. Before serving, place in the refrigerator for at least 30 minutes.

Cucumber and Cream Cheese Roll-Ups

Prep Time: 10 minutes

Ingredients:

- 1 thinly sliced lengthwise cucumber
- 4 ounces (low-fat) cream cheese
- 1 tablespoon chopped fresh dill
- Smoked salmon slices (optional)

1. Arrange the cucumber slices on a level surface.

2. Drizzle each slice with a small amount of cream cheese.

3. Top the cream cheese with chopped dill.

4. If preferred, top with a slice of smoked salmon.

5. Use toothpicks to secure the cucumber slices as you roll them up.

Berry and Almond Smoothie

Prep Time: 5 minutes

Ingredients:

- 1/2 cup of unsweetened almond milk
- 1/4 cup low-fat Greek yogurt
- 1/2 cup mixed berries (blueberries and strawberries)
- 1 tablespoon almond butter
- Ice cubes, if desired

Guidelines:

1. Combine almond butter, Greek yogurt, mixed berries, and almond milk in a blender.

2. Blend until smooth.

3. If you want a cooler consistency, add ice cubes.

4. Transfer to a glass and savor.

Chia Seed Pudding with Mango

Prep Time: 2 hours (mostly inactive)

Ingredients:

- 2 tablespoons chia seeds
- 1/2 cup unsweetened almond milk
- 1/2 teaspoon vanilla extract
- 1/2 cup diced fresh mango

Guidelines:

1. Combine almond milk, vanilla extract, and chia seeds in a bowl.

2. Give it a good stir, then refrigerate for at least 2 hours or overnight to let it thicken.

3. Top with diced mango before serving.

Roasted Chickpeas

Preparation Time: 35 minutes

Ingredients:

- 1 can (15 ounce) rinsed and drained chickpeas
- 1 teaspoon smoked paprika
- 1 tablespoon olive oil
- 1/4 teaspoon cayenne pepper
- 1/2 teaspoon cumin
- Salt to taste

Guidelines:

1. Preheat the oven to 400°F (200°C).

2. Using a paper towel, pat dry chickpeas to absorb any remaining moisture.

3. Combine chickpeas with cumin, cayenne pepper, smoked paprika, salt and olive oil in a bowl.

4. Arrange chickpeas in a single layer on a baking sheet.

5. Roast for 25 to 30 minutes until crispy, stirring the pan halfway through.

Yogurt-Dipped Strawberries

Prep Time: 10 minutes (+ freezing time)

Ingredients:

- 1/2 cup low-fat Greek yogurt
- 1 cup washed and dried strawberries
- 1 tablespoon honey, if desired

Guidelines:

1. Combine Greek yogurt and honey, if using, in a small bowl.

2. Dip each strawberry into the yogurt mixture, covering halfway.

3. Transfer to a parchment-lined tray and refrigerate for 1 to 2 hours.

Cauliflower Popcorn

Preparation Time: 30 minutes

Ingredients:

- 2 cups cauliflower florets
- 1 tablespoon olive oil
- 1/2 teaspoon powdered garlic
- 1/2 teaspoon of powdered onion
- 1/2 tsp. smoked paprika

- To taste, add salt and pepper.

1. Preheat the oven to 425°F (220°C).

2. Toss cauliflower florets with olive oil, garlic powder, onion powder, smoked paprika, salt, and pepper in a bowl.

3. Layer cauliflower in a single layer on a baking pan.

4. Roast until crispy and brown for 20 to 25 minutes.

Pumpkin Spice Chia Pudding

Preparation Time: 2 hours (mostly inactive)

Ingredients:

- 1/2 tablespoon chia seeds
- 1/2 cup unsweetened almond milk
- 1/2 teaspoon pumpkin spice
- 1/4 cup pureed pumpkin
- 1 tablespoon maple syrup

Guidelines:

1. Combine chia seeds, maple syrup, almond milk, pumpkin puree, and pumpkin spice in a bowl.

2. Give it a good stir, then freeze for at least 2 hours or overnight until thicken.

3. Sprinkle additional pumpkin spice on top before serving.

7-Days Meal Plan

Here's a 7-day sample meal plan tailored for individuals managing CKD Stage 3 and Type 2 Diabetes. This plan incorporates the principles of a healing diet, focusing on nutrient balance, portion control, and suitable food choices for kidney health and blood sugar control.

Day 1:

Breakfast: Quinoa Porridge with Fresh Berries

Lunch: Grilled Chicken Salad with Mixed Greens

Snack: Greek Yogurt with a Sprinkle of Chia Seeds

Dinner: Baked Salmon Fillet

Dessert: Sliced Strawberries

Day 2:

Breakfast: Whole Grain Toast with Almond Butter

Lunch: Lentil and Vegetable Soup

Snack: Handful of Almonds

Dinner: Turkey Stir-Fry with Broccoli and Bell Peppers

Dessert: Mixed Berry Parfait for Dessert

Day 3:

Breakfast: Oatmeal with Walnuts and Diced Apple

Lunch: Quinoa Salad with Chickpeas

Snack: Cottage Cheese with Pineapple

Dinner: Grilled Shrimp Skewers

Dessert: Sliced Mango for Dessert

Day 4:

Breakfast: Whole Grain Pancakes with Blueberries

Lunch: Turkey and Avocado Wrap with Whole Wheat Tortilla

Snack: Celery Sticks with Almond Butter

Dinner: Quinoa Pilaf with Mixed Vegetables

Dessert: Fresh Berries Medley

Day 5:

Breakfast: Spinach and Feta Omelette

Lunch: Chickpea and Vegetable Stir-Fry

Snack: Handful of Walnuts

Dinner: Grilled Chicken Breast

Dessert: Kiwi and Strawberry Salad for Dessert

Day 6:

Breakfast: Smoothie Bowl with Mixed Berries and Granola

Lunch: Quinoa and Black Bean Salad

Snack: Cottage Cheese with Berries

Dinner: Steamed Broccoli and Quinoa

Dessert: Fresh Pineapple Chunks for

Day 7:

Breakfast: Whole Grain Waffles with Sliced Strawberries

Lunch: Caprese Salad with Fresh Mozzarella, Tomatoes, and Basil

Snack: Almond and Date Energy Bites

Dinner: Stir-Fried Tofu with Vegetables

Dessert: Mixed Fruit Salad for

This sample meal plan provides a variety of delicious and nutrient-packed options, ensuring individuals with CKD Stage 3 and Type 2 Diabetes can enjoy a diverse and satisfying diet while supporting their health goals. Remember to adapt the plan based on individual preferences, dietary restrictions, and specific nutritional needs.

Chapter 6: Modifications to Lifestyle for Optimal Health

In addition to dietary choices, lifestyle modifications are essential for the management of Type 2 Diabetes and Chronic Kidney Disease (CKD) Stage 3. Taking a holistic approach to wellness entails incorporating healthy practices into many aspects of everyday living, such as exercise, stress reduction, good sleeping practices, and taking adequate water.

Importance of Regular Exercise

Physical activity is a cornerstone of optimal health for individuals managing CKD Stage 3 and Type 2 Diabetes. Frequent exercise promotes cardiovascular health, helps maintain a healthy weight, and improves insulin sensitivity, all of which are factors in general well-being.

Moderate exercise can assist CKD patients control their blood pressure, which is essential for maintaining renal function. Exercises like cycling, swimming, or walking can be customized to individual fitness level and added to a daily routine. Exercise reduces the need for insulin in the management of diabetes by promoting glucose absorption into cells.

Strategies for Stress Reduction

Chronic stress can have significant effects on blood sugar regulation and kidney health. It is crucial to put stress-reduction techniques into practice, such as mindfulness exercises, deep breathing exercises, and meditation. These methods benefit not only mental health but also the physiological reactions associated with diabetes and CKD.

Reducing stress is especially important for individuals with diabetes, since stress hormones can raise blood sugar levels. Using relaxation techniques becomes an important part of a larger diabetes management plan.

Obtaining Adequate Sleep

Quality sleep is a crucial component of good health that is sometimes overlooked. The body heals and regenerates during sleep, influencing both renal and metabolic processes. Individuals managing diabetes and CKD should place a high priority on getting enough sleep.

Insulin resistance has been associated with sleep deprivation, which may exacerbate difficulties associated with diabetes. The link between kidney function and sleep for people with CKD emphasizes how crucial it is to develop regular sleep habits in order to promote general well-being.

Hydration and Its Effects on Diabetes and CKD

One lifestyle choice that has a direct impact on kidney health is drinking enough water. Adequate fluid intake helps maintain blood volume and supports the kidneys in filtering waste. However, individuals with CKD may need to monitor fluid intake more closely, depending on their specific Situation.

Staying hydrated is essential for managing diabetes as well. Maintaining adequate hydration helps regulate blood sugar by averting glucose spikes caused by dehydration. Water is the best beverage choice, and individuals should be mindful of the potential impact of sugary or caffeinated drinks on blood sugar and kidney function.

Conclusion

To sum up, the "**CKD Stage 3 and Diabetes Type 2 Cookbook**" is an extensive and priceless resource for individuals attempting to navigate the difficulties associated with managing these health illnesses. The thoughtfully chosen recipes, lifestyle tips, and dietary recommendations provide a road map for improved health as well as a transformed and vibrant life.

This cookbook offers a comprehensive approach that takes into account the particular needs of people with Type 2 Diabetes and CKD Stage 3, going beyond the scope of conventional dietary guidelines. From understanding the foundations of a healing diet to creating delicious and nutrient-packed recipes, this cookbook empowers individuals to take charge of their health through conscious and informed decisions.

The significance of lifestyle changes cannot be overstated. Embracing the values listed in this cookbook, which include healthy eating, consistent exercise, stress reduction, and enough hydration is a road map for achieving optimal wellbeing rather than just a treatment plan for ailments. Adopting these adjustments can help individuals see improvements in their blood sugar, kidney function, and general health.

As you embark on this culinary journey, remember that each recipe is a step toward reclaiming your health and embracing a life free from the constraints of CKD Stage 3 and Type 2 Diabetes. You have the ability to savor not just the flavors of these meticulously curated meals but the sweet taste of a healthier, more energetic existence.

Encourage yourself to make these adjustments as a celebration of life, health, and the happiness that comes from taking care of your body and soul rather than as a necessity. Each dish you make from this cookbook is an investment in your health and a pledge to a time when maintaining your health will not be a sacrifice but a lifelong companion.

Savor the tastes, enjoy the journey, and let this cookbook serve as your road map to a happier, healthier life. Your body will appreciate it, and the renewed vitality that results from making wellbeing a priority with every meal will lift your soul.

Bon appétit to a life well-lived

Weekly Meal Planner Journal

Dates:

	BREAKFAST	LUNCH	DINNER	SNACKS
MON				
TUE				
WED				
THU				
FRI				
SAT				
SUN				

Shopping list

NOTES

Weekly Meal Planner Journal

Dates:

	BREAKFAST	LUNCH	DINNER	SNACKS
MON				
TUE				
WED				
THU				
FRI				
SAT				
SUN				

Shopping list

_____

_____

_____

_____

_____

NOTES

Weekly Meal Planner
Journal

Dates:

	BREAKFAST	LUNCH	DINNER	SNACKS
MON				
TUE				
WED				
THU				
FRI				
SAT				
SUN				

Shopping list

NOTES

Weekly Meal Planner
Journal

Dates:

	BREAKFAST	LUNCH	DINNER	SNACKS
MON				
TUE				
WED				
THU				
FRI				
SAT				
SUN				

Shopping list

_____
_____
_____
_____
_____

NOTES

Weekly Meal Planner
Journal

Dates:

	BREAKFAST	LUNCH	DINNER	SNACKS
MON				
TUE				
WED				
THU				
FRI				
SAT				
SUN				

Shopping list

_____
_____
_____
_____
_____

NOTES

Weekly Meal Planner
Journal

Dates:

	BREAKFAST	LUNCH	DINNER	SNACKS
MON				
TUE				
WED				
THU				
FRI				
SAT				
SUN				

Shopping list

NOTES

Weekly Meal Planner
Journal

Dates:

	BREAKFAST	LUNCH	DINNER	SNACKS
MON				
TUE				
WED				
THU				
FRI				
SAT				
SUN				

Shopping list

NOTES

Weekly Meal Planner Journal

Dates:

	BREAKFAST	LUNCH	DINNER	SNACKS
MON				
TUE				
WED				
THU				
FRI				
SAT				
SUN				

Shopping list
_____
_____
_____
_____
_____
_____

NOTES

Made in the USA
Monee, IL
30 April 2025

16686081R00056